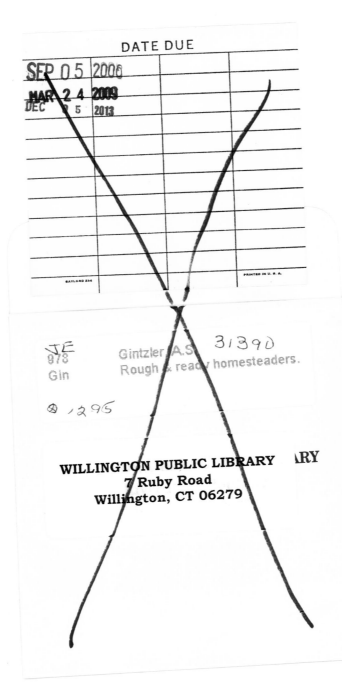

ROUGH & READY
HOMESTEADERS

A. S. GINTZLER

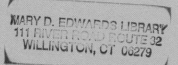
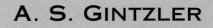

JOHN MUIR PUBLICATIONS
SANTA FE, NEW MEXICO

Acknowledgments

To the homesteaders and their chroniclers.

John Muir Publications, P.O. Box 613, Santa Fe, New Mexico 87504
© 1994 by John Muir Publications
All rights reserved. Published 1994
Printed in the United States of America

First paperback edition. First printing April 1996

Library of Congress Cataloging-in-Publication Data
Gintzler, A. S.
Rough and ready homesteaders / A. S. Gintzler
    p.   cm.
    Includes index.
ISBN 1-56261-233-6
1. Frontier and pioneer life—Great Plains—Juvenile literature. 2. Great Plains—History—
Juvenile literature. [1. Frontier and pioneer life—Great Plains. 2. Great Plains—History.]
I. Title. II. Rough and ready homesteaders.
F596.G56 1994
978—dc20   93-32342
                                                  CIP
                                                  AC

Logo and Cover Design: Paul Perlow
Interior Design and Typography: Linda Braun
Illustrations: Chris Brigman
Printer: Burton & Mayer, Inc.
Title page photo: a horse and bull pulling a
    plow, 1900 © The Bettmann Archive

Distributed to the book trade by
Publishers Group West
Emeryville, California

A prosperous family with their farm tools, 1881

CONTENTS

The Great Plains

The homesteaders made their homes on the Great Plains, a vast grassland smack in the middle of North America. From Texas the Plains swept 2,500 miles north into Canada. From the Missouri River they stretched flat and wide for 400 miles west to the Rocky Mountains.

The land was wild with buffalo and antelope, grizzly bears, wolves, and bobcats. Lizards, opossums, prairie dogs, weasels, pheasants, raccoons, and rattlesnakes made the Plains their home. So did Plains Indians such as the Pawnee, Sioux, Comanche, and Cheyenne. They hunted the buffalo that fed on Plains grasses. These early Plains people were nomads who followed the great herds as they migrated.

The eastern Plains were an ocean of tall prairie grasses. Farther west, the landscape changed. Prairie grasses gave way to shorter matted grasses—and little rainfall. Some areas received less than ten inches of rain a year. The Plains were bathed in sunshine and swept by hot, dry winds.

The Bettmann Archive

A Native American ceremony

"ANTELOPE DOGS"

In prehistoric times, small horses ranged the grasslands of North America. However, these horses died out. In the 1500s, Spanish conquistadors reintroduced the horse to the Great Plains. Native horsemen of the Plains called them "antelope dogs." Horses were well suited to the Plains climate and vegetation. They survived extremes of temperature and fed easily on Plains grasses. Horses could break through winter snow and ice with their hooves to reach the grass below. They moved across the Plains in herds guarding against wolves and bobcats. Until railroads crossed the Plains, horses were the fastest transportation in the West.

Small prehistoric horses once roamed the Plains

GREAT PLAINS

The Great Plains

For these reasons, this immense grassy region was known as the "Great American Desert." It was thought to be unfit for farming or settlement by whites. Explorers and pioneers had crossed the Plains, but they did not stay.

The climate of the Plains was harsh. Temperatures on the northern Plains ranged from 40 below zero in the winter to 117 degrees in the summer. Blinding blizzards raged in the winter and tornadoes hit in the summer. Torrential rains in the spring swelled rivers and hail storms beat the grasses.

Today, the Great Plains cover parts of ten U.S. states and three Canadian provinces. The northern Plains in the U.S. are made up of parts of Montana, Wyoming, and the Dakotas. Colorado, Kansas, and Nebraska are central Plains states. The southern Plains cover parts of New Mexico, Oklahoma, and Texas.

The sea of prairie grass first settled by homesteaders is gone. In its place are wheat fields and cattle ranches, fenced off with barbed wire. Farmers graze sheep and cows on the grasslands and grow alfalfa, barley, oats, rye, and corn. No longer known as the Great American Desert, the Plains are now called the "Breadbasket of the World" because of the huge amounts of grain produced in the region. There are coal deposits in the northern Plains, and the southern Plains yield more oil than any other region of the United States.

The Bettmann Archive

Antelope were once plentiful on the Plains

Before the Homesteaders

Long before Columbus arrived in the New World in 1492, all of North America was home to native peoples and wild animals. But the European explorers and settlers who came after Columbus claimed they owned the land.

The first European settlements were built on the east coast of the North American continent. By the mid-1700s, cities and villages of European settlers dotted this area. Hardy pioneers farmed the surrounding lands.

As European immigrants continued to come to America and raise families, they turned more and more of the eastern wilderness into small farms. Every year thousands of acres of forest were cleared, and the native people were pushed off of their land.

In the mid-1700s, settlers headed west into the Appalachian Mountains. At that time, the British ruled most of the East Coast. By the end of the American Revolution in 1783, pioneer farmers were clearing land as far west as the Mississippi River.

After winning independence from England, the new American government claimed all of the land that the British had claimed east of the Mississippi River. The new government divided up the land that was not yet settled by white people. They offered to sell it to pioneers who wanted new farmlands. But few pioneers in the 1780s had money to buy land. Many ignored the laws and moved onto the unsettled land without paying for it.

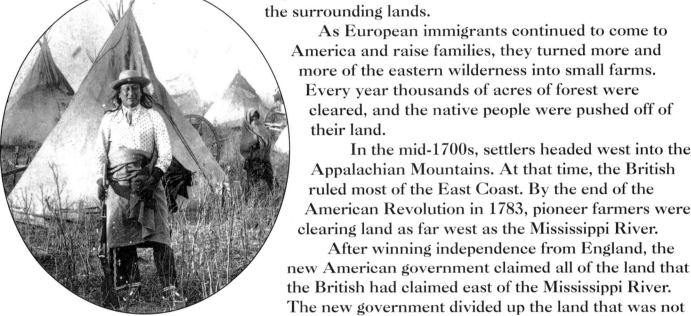

An Oglala Sioux chief, 1891

In 1803 President Thomas Jefferson bought the Louisiana Territory from France. This vast expanse of land included the Great Plains. The Louisiana Territory stretched west of the Mississippi River to the Rocky Mountains and north from what is now Texas all the way to Montana.

The Louisiana Purchase, as the sale came to be called, greatly increased the amount of unsettled land owned by the U.S. government.

The Louisiana Purchase greatly expanded U.S. territory

A wagon train heading west

Explorers such as Lewis and Clark blazed trails across the new land. They were followed by trappers and traders. But few pioneer farmers chose to settle on the vast wild grasslands now known as the Great Plains. During the 1840s, pioneers on the Oregon Trail crossed the Plains to settle farms in the Northwest. In 1849, the first gold seekers rushed across the Plains to California. The Far West, from California to Oregon, was being settled. Meanwhile, the dry, windy Plains were still home to native peoples and buffalo.

The U.S. government believed that the best way to use the Great Plains was to farm it. On the eastern edge of the Plains in Missouri and Iowa, settlers began clearing land and plowing the ground.

Meanwhile, northern and southern states were arguing about slavery. Northerners wanted lands west of the Missouri River to be settled as free states. Southerners wanted western lands open to slavery. As pioneer farmers moved west onto the Plains in Kansas and Nebraska, bloody battles broke out between pro-slavery and anti-slavery settlers.

*Prospectors crossed the Plains
on their way to California*

DIVIDING THE LAND

After the Revolutionary War, the new U.S. government passed a law that encouraged settlers to buy land the government owned. Surveyors mapped out land into squares one mile long on each side. These square-mile pieces were called "sections." Each contained 640 acres of land. Often, sections were further divided into quarter sections of 160 acres each.

Homesteading the Plains

In the 1800s, many Americans believed that the U.S. had a right to own all of the land between the East and West Coasts. For the new country to grow and prosper, they felt the U.S. had to expand west. After the Civil War began in 1861, President Lincoln and Congress urged anti-slavery northerners to settle free states in the West. They passed the Homestead Act in 1862, opening government-owned lands on the Plains to settlement.

The Homestead Act took effect on January 1, 1863, while the Civil War raged back East. It said that, for just $18, any U.S. citizen or immigrant could own 160 acres if he or she agreed to farm the land for five years. To struggling farmers in the eastern U.S. and to poor peasants in Europe, it sounded like a dream come true. The people who bought these land claims from the government were called homesteaders.

At first, few homesteaders settled the Plains. The "Great American Desert" was thought to be too dry for farming. Yet land-hungry homesteaders began riding wagons onto the prairies of eastern Kansas and Nebraska. Rainfall and climate in this tall-grass prairie country helped them to grow wheat. West of the prairie, however, there was little rain. Homesteaders didn't move farther west until changes occurred on the Great Plains.

Crews building the Central Pacific railroad in 1868

The railroads promised good farmland to draw settlers west

Before the homesteaders arrived, the Great Plains were home to millions of wild buffalo. Plains Indians hunted migrating herds, killing only what they needed to survive. The animal's meat and hide provided food, clothing, and shelter. For Plains Indians, buffalo were the source of life and thought to be sacred. But life on the Plains began to change rapidly in the 1860s and 1870s. White hunters killed the buffaloes for their hides and left the meat to rot. Texas cowboys drove herds of cattle through the Plains to railroads in Kansas. Their cows carried disease and competed with the buffalo for food and water. Railroad builders slaughtered buffalo to clear the way for the tracks and to feed the railroad crews. Train passengers shot the animals with high-powered rifles from moving trains. By 1887, fewer than 1,000 buffalo remained from the herds of millions.

The Bettmann Archive

Hunters destroyed whole herds of buffalo

By the 1870s, railroads crossed the Plains and made travel easier. Then in the 1880s, heavy rains swept western Kansas and Nebraska. Railroads and businessmen who owned frontier lands urged farmers to homestead the western part of the Plains. They claimed the western Plains could be farmed easily and that rain would continue to fall. Homesteaders took a chance, riding the railroads and following the rains west.

Filing at the land claims office

The U.S. government had paid the railroads to lay tracks across the country connecting the east and west coasts. Railroad companies also received 150 million acres of free land alongside their tracks. To make money and to keep the trains busy transporting people and freight, the railroad companies began selling this land to homesteaders. They even advertised the available land in Europe. Thousands of European immigrants came to America to buy land on the Plains. Some became prosperous "sodbusters," as early Plains farmers were called. Some went broke and were sorry they ever came.

Trails and Waterways West

The first challenge the homesteaders faced was getting out onto the Plains. Early homesteaders traveled river routes and wagon trails. These routes had been used before by explorers and pioneers heading west for California and Oregon. The homesteader's journey was long and dangerous.

Steamboats carried homesteaders upriver

The Bettmann Archive

Homesteaders took steamboats up the Mississippi and Missouri rivers as far west as they could. These steamboats carried married couples, single men, women, children, missionaries, and gamblers. All were seeking a better life. Some steamboats were clean and roomy, while others were crowded and infested with bed bugs. Often the only place to sleep was on the floor.

Riverboat musicians entertained the passengers with popular tunes like "Clementine." Some of the passengers held prayer meetings while others played poker and gambled with dice. A throw of the dice cost 50 cents. Both men and women tried to win gold, watches, and money. But they were no match for professional riverboat gamblers who easily won against farmers.

These steamboat journeys ended in river towns like Kansas City and St. Joseph, Missouri. From there passengers traveled by stagecoach or covered wagon to their homesteads.

After the Civil War ended in 1865, more and more settlers arrived on the western Plains in search of land to farm. They rode in Consetoga wagons along the Oregon and Mormon trails that followed the Platte River west. Conestoga wagons were called "prairie schooners," because from a distance they looked like sail ships, or schooners.

Conestoga wagons were 25 feet long and weighed about 3,000 pounds. They were pulled by teams of oxen, mules, or horses with names like "Yaller," "Fuss," and "Hairy." Oxen moved very slowly, about two miles an hour. But they were hardy and strong. A good team could travel about 25 miles a day.

Homesteaders often traveled in wagon trains with other families headed west. In the days before road maps, they relied on a guide who rode in front on horseback and led the way. When they came to a stream or river, they had to ford it, crossing through the water. Sometimes their belongings were swept away by the strong currents. At night, homesteaders pulled their wagons into a circle for protection against wild animals, outlaws, and Indians defending their territory.

Homesteaders prepared for weeks or months before setting out on their journey. The women baked bread and packed flour, salted pork, bacon, and beans. The wagon was equipped like a house on wheels. Some even had a wood-burning stove sitting in the middle, with a stovepipe sticking through the wagon top.

Homesteaders packed their wagons so full of food and equipment that there was little room for passengers. Only the weak and very old rode inside during the long journey. Everyone else, even young children, walked alongside.

Fording a river

By the 1880s, homesteaders were riding the railroads west. Journeys that had taken months in wagons took only a few weeks or even days by train. Once train travel became common, wagons were used only to carry families the short distance from the railroad station to their homestead.

IRON RAILS

In the 1880s, the new railroads across the Plains advertised low fares for families, household goods, and livestock. They wanted people to settle the Plains so the railroads could keep busy and make money. Railroads offered homesteaders discounts on special "land exploration" tickets. Settlers could travel west, inspect lands, and return East before packing up the family. This ended the risks of steamboat travel and long overland journeys.

Settlers rode the new railroads west

UPI/Bettmann

9

Who Were the Homesteaders?

The inexpensive land offered by the Homestead Act drew settlers of all kinds to the Great Plains. European immigrants, farmers from Kentucky, former slaves from the South, and many others headed west to claim farmland. Railroad companies hired agents to attract settlers to the west. The railroads expected to profit from land sales and passenger and freight fees. These agents traveled to Europe to urge people to immigrate to America.

The agents lured immigrants with travel brochures that showed beautiful streams, rich farm lands, and tree-lined streets. But the land they were selling was actually dry and swept by hot winds. States and towns also sent agents to Europe and to eastern cities in the United States hoping to draw settlers.

European immigrants were lured to America by ads for cheap land

Poor European villagers and farmers who had little land and food believed the stories of good inexpensive American land. Many formed groups and traveled to the Great Plains together.

Hayes, Kansas, was settled by 108 Russian Catholic families. Grace Valley, Kansas, was founded by 24 families from the Russian Crimea. In northeastern Kansas, colonies were settled by the French and by French-speaking Swiss and Belgians. Scandinavians homesteaded the Dakotas. Groups from Balestrand, Norway, settled communities in Minnesota and Wisconsin. As these communities grew, young couples moved farther west. Norwegians settled Deuel County, South Dakota, after migrating from Minnesota. Immigrants wrote home to the "Old Country" encouraging others to follow.

VEGETARIAN CREEK

A group of vegetarians tried to form a colony near Humboldt, Kansas. They agreed to eat no meat and to live a healthy lifestyle. In the mid-1850s they started building. They had plans for a farming college, a dining hall, and mills. Families arrived in the spring and lived in tents. Work began, but spring rains soon drove the settlers to higher, drier ground. The group scattered and began homesteading free lands on their own. All that remains of the vegetarian colony today is a small stream called Vegetarian Creek.

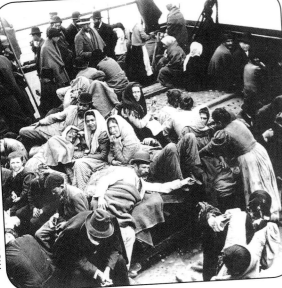

Immigrants on a ship bound for America

Homesteaders from the Bothian Coast of Sweden settled together. Farmers from County Cork, Ireland, settled together in Butte, Montana. Thousands left Norway and Ireland for the Plains. Yugoslav, Finnish, and English farmers became sodbusters in the American West. German-speaking farmers outnumbered all other immigrant groups on the Plains. A group of Germans called the Ebenezers moved from Buffalo, New York, to Kansas.

Many homesteaders from eastern states and the Midwest also came in groups. These American-born settlers looked west for opportunity. Civil War veterans banded together at the Soldiers' Free Homestead Colony in Gibbon, Nebraska. The Ohio Soldiers' Colony homesteaded land in Allen County, Kansas. Seventh-day Baptists established a colony at North Loup, Nebraska.

African American ex-slaves called "Exodusters" began an "exodus" from the South after President Lincoln freed the slaves in 1863. About 8,000 former slaves from Tennessee followed Benjamin Singleton to Kansas. The town of Nicodemus in Graham County, Kansas, was founded by African Americans.

Homesteaders also settled the Plains as individual families. A widow and her three children homesteaded claims together in Kansas. They formed a small village of their own on connected sections of land. It was not uncommon for single women or sisters to file land claims under the Homestead Act. From Texas to Montana, immigrants from many lands tried to make their homes on the Great Plains.

A family outside their sod house in Nebraska

11

The Homesteader's House

Sodbusters did what they could to be comfortable on the Plains. But sod houses offered little comfort. They were small, dark, damp, and dirty. Water poured through the roof when it rained. Snakes and mice burrowed in the walls. They were crude—but they were "home."

Pioneers in the East had built log cabins and wood-frame houses. On the Plains, however, there were few trees to cut for logs. Early homesteaders settled in river valleys and along streams where trees grew. In a short time, however, these choice lands were taken. Later sodbusters had to settle on the higher treeless grasslands. Their building materials were earth and sod.

Two types of homes were built, the sod house and the dugout. Dugouts were the first homes of most settlers on the Plains. They were little more than caves dug into hillsides. The opening of the caves were closed off with 3-foot-long bricks cut from sod, the layer of matted earth formed by grass and plant roots.

Dugouts provided temporary shelter for families of six people or more until a larger home could be built. A dugout with one window, a door, a stove, and several beds of straw cost less than $3 to build.

The larger one-room sod house was made completely of sod bricks. It took half an acre of sod to build a house 16 by 20 feet. Homesteaders built the walls of their houses with sod bricks, filling cracks and spaces with dirt. A flat roof of grass and sod was then laid across the wooden poles that stretched from the top of one wall to the top of the opposite wall.

This earthen roof soon sprouted prairie grasses, wild flowers—and snakes. Snakes and mice lived on the Plains and in the homesteader's sod house. So did flies and grasshoppers.

The Bettmann Archive

This family lived in a dugout, a house dug out of a hill

BUFFALO CHIPS AND TWISTED HAY

Fuel for heating was scarce during the winter. Back East, wood had been plentiful and cheap. But there were few trees on the Plains. So homesteaders followed the example of Plains Indians and burned "buffalo chips," the animals' dung. They also burned the cow chips left behind by passing herds of cattle. But the most plentiful fuel was grass. Homesteaders twisted grass or hay into sticks and burned them. Keeping warm during the long, cold Plains winters took toughness and imagination.

A woman gathering chips with her daughter

Most homesteaders didn't have glass to put in the windows of their houses. Instead, windows were covered with buffalo hides to keep out wind and dust. Rain leaked through ceilings like indoor waterfalls. Homesteaders put pots and pans on the floor to catch the running water. Heavy, rain-soaked roofs sometimes caved in—crushing families. But sod houses stood strong against the wind and didn't burn in prairie fires. And they were warm in the winter and cool in the summer.

Homesteaders built crude furniture from any available wood. They used boxes as tables, chairs, and cupboards. They carpeted their dirt floor with straw and made candles from buffalo fat for light at night. Women wove brooms from coarse grasses, but sod houses could never be swept completely clean. Some homesteaders had rag rugs to give a touch of homespun "finery" to their crude homes.

Water was in short supply on the dry Plains. Homesteaders had to dig deep wells to tap underground water. They never had running water in their houses. They had to haul water in buckets and barrels for use in the home. Nothing came easy for sod house dwellers on the Plains.

Snakes and mice made their nests in sod houses

Farming on the Plains

At first, the homesteaders used farming methods similar to those they had used back East and in Europe. They "busted sod," plowing and turning over the thick, matted carpet of sod that covered the region. Then they planted seeds and relied upon rain to water the crops. This method worked well on the eastern Plains, where rain was plentiful in the 1880s. But on the western Plains, there was not enough rainfall to grow crops this way. Sodbusters needed new farming methods.

A homesteader named Webster Campbell developed a new method of farming in South Dakota called "dry farming." He plowed deeply, then packed down the soil and left a loose cover layer called mulch. This kept moisture near the plant roots. For dry farming to work, the soil had to be tilled, or turned, every time it rained. Campbell took this and other dry farming methods to Nebraska, where the first homesteaders' crops had failed. These farmers had planted seeds brought from back East. Campbell encouraged them to plant crops that needed less water. These crops were known as "drought-resistant."

The Bettmann Archive

A Plains farmer busting sod

HARNESSING THE WIND

Water was scarce on the surface of the dry, windy Plains. But huge lakes of water lay deep underground. The trick was to bring underground water to the surface. A mechanic from Connecticut named Daniel Halloway had a solution to this problem. He began building windmills in 1854. Plains farmers sank wells 300 feet deep to reach water. Windmills with 10-foot long blades were built over the wells. When the wind blew, it turned the blades of the windmill. The turning blades powered a pump that brought well water to the surface. By the 1870s, windmills were a common feature on the Plains.

Windmills were in use by the 1850s

Homesteaders with their horse-drawn reaper

Some farmers also tried irrigation, watering their crops by redirecting the flow of rivers and streams. But this method was costly and not very effective. It worked well only in hilly country and river valleys where water naturally ran downhill to the fields. Less than one percent of Plains lands were irrigated by 1889. Later farmers joined together to build reservoirs and to dig deep water wells.

The invention of new farm machinery also helped the homesteaders. Before the 1870s, hand-held scythes were used to cut grain and grasses. Grain was then separated from the cut stalk by hand.

In the 1870s, harvesting and threshing machines were invented. These large machines were pulled through fields by teams of horses or mules. The harvester cut the stalk of the wheat. The thresher separated the grain from the stalk. With these machines, sodbusters could farm much larger pieces of land.

Homesteaders worked together in crews during harvesting season. They camped out in each other's fields, sleeping on beds of hay. Combines—machines that combined cutting, threshing, and sacking—were in use by the 1880s. About the same time, steam-powered tractors began to replace teams of horses and mules. But many small farmers continued to use horse and mule teams well into the twentieth century.

A horse and bull pull this farmer's plow

By the 1880s, wheat fields on the Great Plains supplied half of the grain for the U.S. More farmers moved to the Plains as the demand for wheat and corn increased worldwide. Plains farmers survived periods of drought and eventually came to supply grain to all parts of the world.

The Hardships of Homesteading

Cheap land lured homesteaders west, but they paid a high price for their dream. Homesteaders faced many hardships on the Plains. Nothing caught them more off guard than the grasshopper invasion of 1874. Grasshoppers arrived on the northern Plains in huge swarms like black clouds 150 miles long and 100 miles wide. Their wings roared like a storm. When they landed, they sometimes piled up over six inches deep. They covered railroad tracks so thickly the trains couldn't push through. Train wheels spun helplessly in the slime of crushed grasshopper bodies.

Homesteaders called these grasshoppers "Rocky Mountain locusts" because they ate through everything in their path. They stripped wheat crops to the ground in minutes. Home gardens were devoured. Hungry "hoppers" even ate the wooden handles off of farm tools. Tree limbs snapped under their weight. Farmers whose crops were destroyed by the hoppers either dug in and planted again, or left in defeat.

Homesteaders faced other problems too. For many years before homesteaders arrived, ranchers had driven and grazed cattle on the Great Plains. They didn't own the grasslands, but they used them freely. Cattle ranchers hated homesteaders who came to settle, farm, and fence the land.

Grasshoppers stripped crops to the ground within minutes

The cattlemen found ways to claim the best water supplies and the best grasslands. Homesteaders were left with the driest lands. Ranchers drove their herds over farmers' lands, trampling crops, and Texas longhorn cattle spread disease to farmers' cows.

The Plains climate was tough on homesteaders. The rains of the 1880s did not last. In 1889, drought struck the western regions of Kansas, Nebraska, and the Dakotas. Hot winds tore across the Plains, scorching crops. There was no rain again in 1890. Many farms were ruined. Broke and hungry homesteaders packed up and returned east. Counties and towns were deserted as farmers, merchants, and businessmen fled the heat.

A Conestoga wagon caught in a windstorm

Some stayed, however, determined to make a living on the Plains. They were in for hard times. Drought struck again in 1893 and every year until 1897. Hail storms also destroyed crops. Years of harsh winters tested the homesteaders' endurance. As their crops failed year after year, many once-hopeful sodbusters were forced to desert their farms and return to the East.

Even during good times, life on the sod frontier was difficult. Sod houses were bleak and dirty. They were separated from other homes and towns by miles of prairie. Homesteaders were often lonely.

Prairie fires were also a constant threat on the dry, windy Plains. Lightning, sparks from a gun, or a smoldering campfire could start a blaze. Fires rushed across the grasslands with the wind. Homes and barns burned to the ground. Livestock were roasted alive. Entire farms were lost. The town of Leola, South Dakota, was almost burned to the ground.

About half the homesteaders in most counties eventually left, "busted and disgusted." But a steady stream of others kept coming from the East.

BLINDING BLIZZARDS

Winter blizzards tore across the Plains. Homesteaders had to bring their farm animals into their houses to keep them from freezing to death. The blizzard of 1888 trapped so many children at their schools that it is remembered as "the school children's storm." During the winter of 1880 to 1881, snow blocked the Dakota railroads for 79 days. It piled 11 feet high. Blizzards blinded homesteaders as they stepped out the door. Families were lost and frozen in their own yards.

Winter storms were among the hardships homesteaders faced

Native Peoples of the Plains

Native Americans had been living on the Great Plains for centuries before the homesteaders arrived. The Sioux, Cheyenne, Pawnee, Comanche, and other Plains Indian tribes hunted great migrating herds of buffalo on foot and later on horseback.

Plains Indians built their homes and made robes and shoes from buffalo hides. They made tools from buffalo bones and thread from the sinew, the tissue that connects muscle to bone. The buffalo was considered sacred and no part was wasted.

Because the buffalo was the source of life for the Plains Indians, tribes sometimes fought over hunting grounds. Yet they all shared a way of life that left the Plains mostly undisturbed.

White settlement of the Plains changed this way of life forever. Before the Revolutionary War, British law did not allow white settlement in the West. The government feared that settlers would clash with the Indians in all-out war. After independence was won, the new U.S. government also discouraged westward expansion.

The Bettmann Archive

Cherokees marching to Oklahoma on the "Trail of Tears"

Then in 1830, the government changed its mind. It passed the Indian Removal Act, which paved the way for white settlement west of the Mississippi River. Native Americans were forced into what was called Indian Territory. This was the land that would later become Kansas, Nebraska, and Oklahoma.

More than thirty eastern tribes were moved to Kansas and Nebraska. The Choctaws were driven out of their Mississippi homeland. The Cherokees were pushed out of Georgia to Oklahoma. Of the 15,000 Cherokees who were forced to make the 116-day journey on foot, 4,000 died. The ordeal came to be called the "Trail of Tears."

The government promised Native Americans that they could own these western lands "as long as the rivers shall run and the grass shall grow." But the promise was soon broken.

INDIAN WARS

By the 1860s, cattlemen, gold seekers, and homesteaders were rushing over the Plains, the homelands of many native peoples. Next came the railroad. Railroad builders killed the Indians' sacred buffalo for meat and to make room for the railroad. The U.S. government began a campaign of "Indian Wars" to remove Native Americans from areas whites wanted to settle. Guns, starvation, and disease were the weapons. Sioux Chief Red Cloud, Chief Joseph of the Nez Percé, and other Indian leaders fought back. Indians defeated General George Custer at the Battle of Little Bighorn, but lost at Wounded Knee. The Native American struggle for sovereignty, which means the right to self-government, continues today.

The Bettmann Archive

Chief Joseph

Fur traders and gold diggers took over native lands. Pioneer farmers pushed west onto the eastern Plains. By 1850, Indian lands in Oregon were opened to white settlement. Kansas and Nebraska were opened in 1854. Tribes were pushed into Oklahoma.

The Homestead Act of 1862 allowed whites to settle for good on the Plains. Plains Indians felt invaded and angry. Homesteaders and Indians clashed. Most homesteaders viewed Native Americans as uncivilized and called them "savages." Most Native Americans wanted nothing to do with whites, but there were exceptions.

Some tribes let whites homestead on Indian lands for a fee of about $10. In Humboldt, Kansas, homesteaders traded pork and watermelons with Indians for buffalo meat. German immigrants in Kansas traded wine and bread. Some Indians learned to speak German.

Other native tribes, such as the Sioux, Comanche, and Apache, resisted white settlers, gold seekers, and the U.S. Army. But the flood of white settlers couldn't be stopped. By 1889, even Oklahoma's Indian Territory was open to homesteaders, and most Native Americans had died of diseases brought by white people, been killed, or been forced onto reservations.

A Cheyenne family outside their home, 1890

The Range Wars

Bloody "Range Wars" in the late 1880s pitted homesteaders against wealthy cattlemen. Quarrels flared up over land and water rights on the Plains. Many people were part of these Range Wars—ranchers, cowboys, sheepherders, and farmers. It wasn't always clear who was in the right.

In the 1870s, cattlemen grazed and drove their herds on the open, unfenced grasslands that stretched from Mexico to Canada. By the mid-1880s, nearly 8 million cattle fed on the wild Plains grasses. Ranching was big business. Wealthy ranchers known as "cattle barons" grazed their herds on both private and public lands. They believed the Great Plains was cattle country. And they fought anyone who disagreed.

A log and sod house in North Dakota

When homesteaders arrived on the Plains, they bought lands that the ranchers had used for grazing their cattle. Cattlemen called them "nesters" and hated them for "nesting," or settling, on the Plains. Around this time, barbed wire was invented. Homesteaders began fencing their land to keep out the cattlemen's herds. Cattlemen in turn began fencing their range lands. They ran barbed wire around watering holes and claimed public lands as their own. They meant to keep out homesteaders, sheepherders, and small ranchers.

Most small ranchers got their start as cowboys working for large ranchers. They rounded up cattle and drove them to market. These working cowboys slowly put together their own herds. But the giant cattle ranches didn't want their hired cowboys going into business for themselves. They wanted to limit competition. They suspected cowboys of cattle "rustling," or stealing. In many cases, they were right.

The Bettmann Archive

Cattlemen ambushing a sheepherder and his flock

Cattle barons also organized against sheepherders who were settling the Plains. They claimed that sheep destroyed the grazing lands. Powerful cattlemen formed groups to protect their lands and water supplies. They began battling the homesteaders, small-time ranchers, and sheepherders. The Range Wars had begun.

Wyoming's Johnson County War in 1892 was a clash of interests. Cattle barons organized to keep small-time ranchers and homesteaders from their lands. They lynched a homesteader named James Avrell, then went after others. They put together a cattlemen's army of gunmen called the Invaders.

Cowboys joined with sodbusters in Johnson County to stop the cattle barons. The groups fought at the TA Ranch. Three days later, the U.S. Cavalry arrived to stop the fighting.

Conflict also erupted in Custer County, Nebraska, when homesteaders cut fences and built homes on grazing lands of the Brighton Ranch. A rancher named Robert Olive was killed. Cattlemen took revenge and hanged two homesteaders.

In Sherman County, Kansas, in 1886, homesteaders organized to stop cattle from trampling their crops. They killed and butchered cows that strayed onto their farms. Similar fights occurred in counties throughout the Plains. But times were changing. By the late 1880s, the cattle kingdom of the Plains had ended. The open range cattle industry finally gave way to farms and smaller ranches.

BARBED WIRE

Homesteaders had neither wood nor stone for fence building. They tried smooth wire fences, but cattle busted through them and trampled their fields. In the 1870s, businessmen came up with the idea of attaching sharp wire barbs to the smooth wire. Cattle shied away from the barbs, and barbed wire was inexpensive to produce. About 400 brands of barbed wire were tested in the 1870s. The twisted double-strand design of Joseph Glidden was the most widely used. Barbed wire fences still border pastures and fields on the Plains today.

Ranchers sometimes cut down the homesteaders' fences

Law and Disorder on the Frontier

Justice on the plains frontier was swift—but not always fair. The western territories were far from the courts and law officers back East. Poor, struggling farm communities on the Plains didn't have real courtrooms and jails. Prisoners were kept locked up in attics and often escaped.

Frontier judges and lawyers had little legal experience. Trials were held in land offices, hotels, barber shops, and under hanging trees. Innocent men were often hanged.

The most hated criminal on the frontier was the horse thief. On the vast, wild plains, horses were valued higher than a man's life. There was a reason for this. A man on horseback had transportation through the wilderness. A man on foot had little chance of survival. He was prey to wild animals, outlaws, and Indians angry about white settlement. Horse stealing was considered to be as bad as—or even worse than—murder. Gangs of horse thieves roamed the countryside.

Members of gangs were sometimes respected citizens who kept their identities secret. One such gang hung out between the towns of Winfield and Wichita in Kansas. In 1870, they drove 250 stolen mules to Texas. But a group of vigilantes from Winfield rode out to stop them. Vigilantes were community members who took the law into their own hands. The Winfield vigilantes ambushed the gang, shot some, and hanged others.

The horse thief was the most hated criminal on the frontier

HOLD-UPS AND HANGINGS

The six-shooter ruled the West. Bandits roamed the trails and held up homesteaders. Wagons were looted, lifesavings stolen, and homesteaders killed. To guard against roving outlaws, homesteaders formed settlers organizations. In Nebraska's early days, pioneer farmers united to battle horse thieves. A hired posse of ten riders would ride out after the outlaws. Six cattle thieves were caught in Rising Sun, Kansas, after killing a farmer. They were hanged to death from the same tree limb.

After the Civil War, a gang called the Jayhawkers raided homesteaders from the South. Jayhawkers claimed to be veterans of the Union Army, but they were just horse thieves. A group of vigilantes, called a posse, tracked the Jayhawkers down and hanged them.

Gunfighters battle on a Kansas street

Vigilantes had no legal authority to use force or arrest people. They were just organized mobs of angry citizens seeking justice. They were hot-headed and suspicious. A stranger riding into town was distrusted. An argument in a saloon could lead to a hanging. Men accused of horse thieving were seldom given a chance to prove their innocence in a fair trial. Sometimes even when trials were held, vigilante juries simply ignored the evidence and hanged innocent men.

In addition to horse thieving, there were arguments over land ownership on the frontier. In one case, a homesteader left his house and land for the winter. When he returned in April, another man had stolen his property and moved into his house. This practice was known as "claim jumping."

Some land thieves were very skilled. Professional claim jumpers often sold land they didn't own. Lawyers represented homesteaders in disagreements over land claims—and made from $300 to $1,200 a month doing it. That was a lot of money in those days.

An outlaw at the gallows

In makeshift courtrooms, lawyers argued with words and fought with fists. Drunken lawyers, judges, and juries debated a man's innocence or guilt. Courts were like circuses. Citizens came from miles around to hear lawyers argue their cases. The spectacle of a hanging always attracted a crowd. Law and order on the frontier were often more about entertainment than justice.

Frontier Towns

Even before the Homestead Act of 1862, towns were "booming" on the eastern Plains. Businessmen back East bought town sites in Nebraska and Kansas. They divided the unsettled land into vacant lots, then sold the lots for a profit. Some lots were given away free to churches and to lottery winners.

Towns sprung up overnight like weeds on the Plains. The town of Lawrence, Kansas, was built in just sixty days. Leavenworth, Kansas, attracted 800 people in its first eight months. It had hotels, blacksmith shops, and clothing stores. Nebraska City and Omaha boomed with settlers.

Hundreds of other towns suddenly appeared on maps of the Kansas and Nebraska territories. But many of these towns existed on paper only. They had no buildings and no people. Advertisements showed tree-lined streets and homes where nothing existed but wild grasses. The only inhabitants of Fairview, Nebraska, and Whitfield, Kansas, were prairie dogs.

Wagon trains arriving at a Plains town

Businessmen advertised these "towns" hoping to get rich off the settlers. Often, their schemes failed. In a short time, even the town names were forgotten.

During the 1870s, towns boomed again on the Plains—this time for real and for good. Homesteaders were putting down roots on the frontier. A flour mill built on a river could boom into a town, like Crete, Nebraska, did. Other towns began as railroad depots and grew into commercial centers. Junction City, Kansas, grew in this way. Some towns faded when the railroad passed them by.

An Oklahoma general store

HOMETOWN PRESS

Frontier town newspapers often started printing even before the first settlers arrived. Towns attracted homesteaders by starting a hometown press. These frontier newspapers were town "boosters." They praised life in the town and hoped to draw more settlers to the area. The *Winfield Courier* declared, ". . . come to Winfield. No better or more desirable place can be found in the state of Kansas." Every town had its *Mainstreet Bugle* or *Enquirer* or *Herald*. Newspapers on the sod frontier made good reading and decent wallpaper.

Frontier newspapers were proud of their home towns

Railroads and homesteaders kept pushing west in the 1880s. Land-hungry settlers followed the rails to unsettled regions. They got off the trains by the hundreds. Dusty main streets were crowded with their wagons and belongings. Homesteaders mobbed the land offices. Railroad towns such as Garden City, Kansas, and Polk, Nebraska, served the needs of homesteaders.

Newspapermen outside their office in Hays City, Kansas

As regions were settled, towns became centers of homesteader commerce. Sodbusters hauled their grain to sell in town. They bought harnesses for their teams, farm equipment, and bottles of medicine. Women purchased fabrics and household goods in the general store.

Every town had one or several saloons. But saloons on the sod frontier were tame compared to those in cattle towns such as Dodge City, Kansas. The homesteader was not as rowdy as the cowboy. He didn't drink to get drunk and raise a ruckus. He was more likely to pass time at the livery stable or sip a bottle of Hostetter's Bitters—a "medicinal" whiskey—at the frontier drug store.

The livery stables were a popular place to catch up on local gossip. Stables rented horses, coaches, and wagons to travelers, land buyers, and agents. Liverymen knew the "comings and goings" of people and the latest news about town.

Towns connected sodbusters on isolated homesteads to a frontier community and to the world back East. Some, such as Lincoln, Nebraska, and Topeka, Kansas, went on to become state capitals.

African American Homesteaders

After the Civil War ended in 1865, slaves were emancipated, or freed, in the South. Yet they had few rights and no political power. Former slave owners controlled local and state governments. Ex-slaves were robbed of their property, beaten, and even lynched. In Kentucky, Tennessee, Louisiana, Mississippi, and Texas, former slaves looked to the West for freedom. They hoped for a better life on the American frontier.

In 1879, some 20,000 to 40,000 African Americans began heading west. Inspired by the biblical "exodus" from slavery, these former slaves were called "Exodusters." They were looking for their own "promised land" on the Great Plains.

Entire families and communities traveled up the Mississippi River and along the cattle trails to Kansas. Former slaves Henry Adams and Benjamin Singleton led the mass movement. Throughout the South, black communities formed groups to fund and organize Exodusters. Homestead associations printed posters and notices advertising the exodus. One poster read, "Ho for Kansas! Brethren, Friends, and Fellow Citizens!"

Many African Americans left the South for a better life

But white southerners tried to stop the Exodusters from leaving. Fearing the loss of cheap labor, former slave owners tried to make their ex-slaves stay. Mississippi steamboat captains refused to allow African Americans on their boats. Some Exodusters were killed or maimed and their leaders jailed. But the exodus continued.

Kansas was the main destination. The famous abolitionist John Brown had lived there. (An abolitionist was a person who worked to abolish, or end, slavery.) As early as 1877, freed slaves were settling in Kansas. In just two months of 1879, some 6,000 African Americans reached the territory. From 1879 to 1880, an estimated 20,000 reached Kansas and Missouri.

Homesteaders with their prairie schooner

At first, the Kansas governor welcomed these new settlers. Black communities with names like Juniper Town and Rattlebone Hollow were founded near existing Kansas towns. The people of Kansas collected $100,000 in relief money to help the Exodusters get settled.

The welcome didn't last long, however. The river town of Leavenworth, Kansas, refused to allow boats bearing former slaves to land. Some 150 Exodusters from Mississippi were driven out of Lincoln, Nebraska. Even the Kansas Pacific Railroad tried to discourage the exodus. Still, the exodus continued.

After establishing communities, Exodusters encouraged others back home to join them. In Colorado, a former slave named Clara Brown sponsored 34 family members and others for passage west. Black soldiers in the West sometimes stayed to homestead after they finished their period of service.

African American homesteaders settled isolated farming communities in Kansas, Nebraska, and Texas. They also settled in Nevada, Utah, and the Pacific Northwest. In Custer County, Nebraska, African American homesteaders built sod houses and worked the land—this time for themselves. By the 1890s, sons and daughters of Nebraska Exodusters were graduating from local high schools and colleges. By 1910, almost a million African Americans lived in Texas and Oklahoma.

NICODEMUS, KANSAS

As early as 1877, former slaves from Kentucky and Tennessee founded a town in Graham County, Kansas. They called it Nicodemus, after an African slave who had bought his freedom. Among the first homesteaders at Nicodemus were the Smiths, Garlands, and Napews. These families spent their first winter in dugout shelters. Their first crops failed, but the homesteaders stayed. By 1880, Nicodemus had a population of 700. In 1883, the state auditor for Kansas was an African American from Nicodemus. Today, with a population of 50, Nicodemus is the only remaining Exoduster settlement on the Plains.

Nicodemus grew to 700 people by 1880

Women on the Plains

The first women on the Great Plains were Native Americans living in tribal villages. Before the homesteaders came west, few white women lived on the Plains. In 1860, only 5 percent of the gold rush population in Nevada and Colorado were women. Ten years later, only 10 percent of the non-Indian populations in Montana, Idaho, and Wyoming were women.

By 1880, however, the West was changing. For the first time, non-Indians put down roots. Homesteaders came to farm the land, build homes, and raise families. Women shared in the work—and the struggle.

Homesteads on the Great Plains were like islands in a sea of grass. The landscape was wide and completely the same for miles—grass and more grass. The hardships of homesteading included heavy winds, intense heat and cold, grasshopper invasions, Indian attack—and loneliness.

On isolated farms, loneliness hit women the hardest. Back East in New England or in more settled regions of the frontier, women had family, friends, and the comforts of home. But on the vast grasslands of the Plains, women homesteaders were marooned like shipwrecked sailors.

Plains men had more mobility. They traveled to distant town markets and mills where they socialized with other farmers while doing business. The women, however, were stranded at home with chores and children. Their lives were often dreary.

Pioneer women often tended to the farm animals

WOMEN ON THEIR OWN

In 1871, land was opened to settlement in Gage County, Nebraska. The first applicant to file was a woman. Many single women homesteaded their own claims. The four Chrisman sisters of Goheen Settlement, Nebraska, owned close to 2,000 acres. Each sister held three 160-acre claims under three different land laws. Women had greater independence in the West than they did back East. By 1869, women in Wyoming Territory could vote, hold public office, and serve on juries. In 1870 in South Pass City, Esther Morris became the first woman justice of the peace in the U.S.

In the 1800s, male and female work roles were very separate. A woman's place was thought to be in the home. But the homesteaders' crude sod houses weren't like the frame houses back East. They had dirt floors and leaky roofs. Flies buzzed night and day, and snakes fell from the ceilings. Howling winds blew dust through the glass-less windows. Sod houses were impossible to keep clean. Some women went crazy trying.

Frontier women with their household tools outside their log cabin

Blizzards in the winter and floods in the spring and summer isolated women even more. Childbirth was often an ordeal. Sometimes it was impossible for a doctor or midwife to get to a distant homestead in time. Many women died in labor or after giving birth.

Plains women made everything from scratch—soap, brooms, candles, clothes. They tended home gardens, spun wool, did all the cooking and housework, cared for the children, and raised pigs, sheep, turkeys, and chickens. The constant work wore some women out. Others, it made stronger.

One woman homesteader in Nebraska planted ten acres of pumpkins, melons, and garden vegetables. She cut saplings to build a pen for her pigs and pickled a 40-gallon barrel of cucumbers. In Wyoming, Elinore Stewart worked a mowing machine as well as any man. She cooked at night, milked seven cows a day, cut hay, and canned dozens of pints of jelly.

The homestead woman had no modern conveniences. She was a hardy survivor on the sod frontier.

Women shopping at a country store

Day to Day Living

Life on the Plains was raw and hard. Women, men, and children all tended to chores. Girls did the work of women, and boys helped their fathers.

On the sod frontier, even the simplest tasks took time and effort. Washing clothes, for example, took two days. Women spread the clothes over rocks near a stream and pounded out the dirt with mallets. Then they rinsed them in the stream.

Homesteaders ate a simple diet. Corn was the most common food on the frontier. Plains women cooked it in more than thirty ways. They made pots of cornmeal mush sweetened with molasses for breakfast. They husked it and boiled it on the cob or rubbed off the kernels to make hominy. Kernels were dried and ground into meal for cornbread, cakes, muffins, and pancakes. Cornbread topped with molasses filled the hungry bellies of Plains children and adults.

The Bettmann Archive

A frontier grocery store in 1890

In the winter, Plains men hunted game. The winter freeze kept the meat from spoiling. Deer, wild turkey, elk, and buffalo meat were a welcome change from corn. Some meat was cut into strips and dried into jerky. Plains Indians had been drying buffalo meat and venison (deer meat) for centuries. Homesteaders also used the animal hides to make robes, pants, shirts, and window coverings.

In the spring, Plains men plowed and planted their fields. Sodbusters were sometimes called "clod hoppers," because they had to hop over clods of busted sod behind their plows. They dug wells and tended their crops. In the fall, they harvested, threshed, and prepared their grain for the mill.

A farmer sometimes traveled 20, 30, or even 100 miles to the nearest mill. He followed trails marked by wooden poles or rags tied to tall weeds. While he was gone—sometimes for a whole week—his neighbors looked after his fields and livestock. His wife tended to the home and guarded against intruders. She knew how to use a gun.

SCHOOL DAYS

Soon after settling the Plains, homesteaders built schools for their children. Communities held school-building bees and everyone helped. The first school in Kansas opened in 1855. Parents paid $1 a month for each child's tuition. One-room schoolhouses were made of sod or logs and had dirt floors. Roofs leaked miserably when it rained. Children sat on benches and had wooden planks for desks. Most schools had fewer than twenty students. They learned the "3 R's"—"reading, writing, and 'rithmetic." There were no blackboards, maps, standard textbooks—or tests.

A one-room schoolhouse

Women sometimes went with their husbands to town. They visited the general store to buy or trade for household goods. While they were gone, neighbors cared for their children as well as their homestead.

"Neighborliness," or community help, was common on the sod frontier. Neighbors held "bees," or gatherings, to help build a family's home, plow their fields, or husk their corn. Women held quilting and sewing bees. Bees were an opportunity to help a neighbor and socialize at the same time.

Lonely homesteaders welcomed any chance to socialize. Dances were held in barns and homes, on wood floors or dirt ground. Any excuse was good for a dance—a wedding, or the welcoming of new neighbors, or the finishing of a house.

Day to day life on the sod frontier was work and more work. But homesteaders took some time out to visit with friends and neighbors. Both work and play were necessary for survival on the Plains.

The Bettmann Archive

Pitching in to help harvest hay

31

Homestead Diaries and Letters

The vast, treeless plains of the western territories were strange to settlers from the forested East. In letters to family and friends in the eastern states, homesteaders wrote of their experiences and struggles.

Howard Ruede settled on the Kansas plains in 1877. In his diaries and letters, Ruede described his early struggles:

April 17, 1877
Made fire and got me some dinner. Bill of fare—mush and broiled ham. The meat flies have got at it, and it must be used soon. Send me a recipe for making johnny cakes. . . . This is not a hightoned way of living. . . . People who live in sod houses . . . are pestered with swarms of bedbugs. . . . Another nuisance here is what people call "Kansas itch," which attacks nearly everybody within a short time.

Under the Homestead Act, land claims were limited to 160 acres. But family members often staked claims side by side to increase their farmlands. Homesteaders wrote to relatives back home, encouraging them to come west. In 1908, a young farmer named Henry Morgenstern wrote to his father and brothers:

September 29
I have been up to the land of which I sent you the papers. . . . I will send you $100 and I want you and Frank to come as soon as you can. I could buy a team and meet you. . . . A person must be here to file and the land won't last long. . . . The land is all level . . . and very easily cleared. No rock. There are about 50 who have located there already and some are building.

In 1909, Elinore Pruitt Stewart became a homesteader in Burnt Fork, Wyoming. In a letter to a friend back in Denver, she told of her trip out West:

A victim of the "Kansas itch"

April 18, 1909
I was twenty-four hours on the train and two days on the stage, and oh, those two days! The snow was just beginning to melt and the mud was about the worst I ever heard of. . . . The road, being so muddy, was full of ruts and the stage acted as if it had the hiccoughs. . . . I have not filed on my land yet because the snow is fifteen feet deep on it. . . . They have just three seasons here, winter and July and August.

A homesteading family beside their Conestoga wagon

Hamlin Garland was a popular Plains writer. In his memoirs, he described how "land fever" struck in Iowa—and neighbors rushed west.

The movement of settlers toward Dakota had now become an exodus, a stampede. Hardly anything else was talked about as neighbors met one another on the road or at the Burr Oak school-house on Sundays. Every man who could sell out had gone west or was going. . . . Farmer after farmer joined the march to Kansas, Nebraska, and Dakota.

MEMORIES OF FIRE

Prairie fires started suddenly and spread quickly. A cinder from a passing train could light dry grasses in an instant. As a girl on a Kansas homestead, Adela Orpen witnessed several fires. She wrote in her memoirs:

'You don't know where you are nor where the house is. Everything is black. Your throat is full of ashes and you can hardly breathe. . . . If you call to your nearest pal on the back firing line, the chances are that he or she has moved away, and may be half a mile distant. You may feel as if you were the last survivor in a horrible world of cinders and blackness. . . .

Prairie fires were a hazard to the homesteaders

Songs of the Sodbusters

Homesteaders told the story of their struggles on the frontier in song. They sang their homespun tunes on the trails west, in sod shanties, and at dances and picnics. Sometimes with a touch of humor, homesteaders complained about the tough times on the Plains, as in this song, "O Dakota Land."

Museum of New Mexico

A frontier family, with their cow on top of their sod dugout

*We've reached the land of desert sweet,
Where nothing grows for man to eat,
The wind it blows with feverish heat,
Across the Plains so hard to beat.*

*O Dakota land, sweet Dakota land,
As on thy fiery soil I stand,
I look across the Plains,
And wonder why it never rains.*

*We have no wheat, we have no oats,
We have no corn to feed our shoats,
Our chickens are so very poor,
They beg for crumbs outside the door.*

The crude sod house was a product of the Plains. It is comically described in this sodbuster version of the old popular song, "The Little Old Log Cabin in the Lane."

*I am looking rather seedy now while holding down my claim,
And my victuals aren't always served the best,
And the mice play shyly round me, as I nestle down to rest,
In my little old sod shanty in the West.*

*The hinges are of leather and the windows have no glass,
While the board roof lets the howling blizzards in,
And I hear the hungry coyote as he slinks up through the grass,
Round my little old sod shanty on my claim.*

Cowboys and homesteaders were rivals on the Plains. In the end, it was the cowboy who left and the farmer who stayed. "The Wyoming Nester" tells the cowboy's point of view.

*Here's luck to all you homesteaders,
You've taken this country at last,
And I hope you'll succeed in the future,
As the cowboys done in the past.*

*Cowboys gathered around
the chuck wagon*

*You've homesteaded all of this country,
Where the slicks and the mavericks
did roam.
You've driven me far from my country,
Far from my birthplace and home.*

Homesteader songs told of hard times, but they also held out hope. African American Exodusters were inspired by a spiritual song or poem about a former slave, Nicodemus. In 1877, Exodusters settled the town of Nicodemus in the Solomon Valley. In an advertisement for more settlers, town founders printed the lyrics to the song-poem, "Nicodemus."

*Nicodemus was a prophet, at least he was as wise,
For he told of the battles to come.
How we trembled with fear, when he rolled up his eyes,
And we heeded the shake of his thumb.*

*Good time coming, good time coming,
Long, long time on the way.
Run and tell Elijah to hurry up Pomp,
To meet us under the cottonwood tree,
In the Great Solomon Valley,
At the first break of day.*

PITCHFORK SERENADE

Entertainment on the sod frontier was often homespun. Communities organized dances, and folks made their own music. Larger towns hired small orchestras and some towns had their own brass bands. A good fiddler could pick up extra cash playing square dances and "hoedowns." In small communities, musicians played whatever instruments they could get their hands on. In 1874 at a dance in Niobrara, Nebraska, musicians played on drums, a fiddle, a pitchfork, and a keg of beer.

A down-home band

Frontier Games and Celebrations

Work and lots of it filled the lives of homestead families. There was little time for fun and games. But there were holidays and breaks in the routine. At the end of long, hot summer days, men and boys splashed in water holes and buffalo wallows. Boys and girls went to parties where they sang rhymes and played ring games like "Skip to My Lou."

Young men courted young women any chance they got. Couples took buggy rides on the prairie. When water holes froze over, skating parties were held on the ice. Boys played hockey with tree branches and girls played tag.

After long work days, families played checkers, cards, and dominoes by candlelight, or they read. Children did homework and studied their "spellers," schoolbooks with spelling words in them. Fathers and mothers read almanacs and the Bible. Some wrote in diaries by lantern light. In the few moments of rest they had, homesteaders entertained themselves and each other.

Going to the town fair

Fourth of July picnics and barbecues were especially festive events. Entire towns took part in the celebration. In Blue Springs, Nebraska, in 1859, townspeople began planning their town party two months ahead of time. They formed committees to catch catfish, collect firewood, and build shelters.

On the big day, they fried more than a thousand pounds of catfish in skillets. Women baked pies, cakes, and breads and brought jams, puddings, and fruits and vegetables from their gardens. Sodbusters came from far-away homesteads and stayed for several days.

Lonely homesteaders joined clubs and lodges to socialize. Women joined sewing circles and church groups. Men belonged to fraternal societies such as the Sons of Malta Lodge. Some lodges were formed for special purposes—like the Anti-Horse Thief Association. Towns organized community theaters and put on plays.

Community dances were attended by everyone—men, women, and children of all ages. Balls, receptions, and fancy "hops" were announced and reported in town newspapers. Women made their own calico dresses and scarves for "calico balls."

BASEBALL ON FRONTIER SOD

Baseball was already being played during the Civil War. After the war, veterans and other homesteaders brought the game to the Great Plains. Baseballs were made at home from old sock yarn, wrapped tight and covered with old boot leather. By the 1870s, many frontier towns had their own teams. Milford, Nebraska, had a team called the Blue Belts, and Oakdale had the Striped Stockings. Towns also sponsored little leagues, called "bantam" leagues, for boys. Wichita, Kansas, had a women's ball club in 1873.

Many frontier towns had their own baseball teams

Horse races drew large crowds on the Plains. Men gathered to bet on the fastest horses in the county. About a thousand sodbusters attended Saturday races at the track near Wichita, Kansas. But horse races could happen anywhere, anytime. Farmers on horseback challenged neighbors or passing strangers to race. Small local races were advertised by word of mouth. Toiling sodbusters were glad for the break from work—and the chance to gamble.

Homesteaders also bet on foot races. Farm boys strove to be the fastest barefoot racers around. Towns challenged each other and put their fastest runners to the test. There were also broad jump and high jump contests.

Other sports, such as roller skating, croquet, and wrestling, found their way to the sod frontier. Many towns had pool tables, which were very popular with players. Nebraska City had two bowling alleys. Homesteaders worked hard and played hard. They plowed fields, pitched hay— and baseballs.

Foot races were a popular form of entertainment

Traveling Salesmen and Entertainers

Isolated homestead families had little contact with the outside world. The Plains were flat and wide and far from the "civilized" East. Frontier towns were 20, 30, or 100 miles from the homestead. A broken clock stayed broken for weeks or months. Aches and pains were treated with home remedies or not at all. The sod frontier was therefore ripe for traveling businesses of all kinds.

Peddlers, medicine sellers, and entertainers rode from homestead to homestead and from town to town. They brought goods and services to frontier families. But sodbusters were often swindled, or cheated, by these travelers. By the time a farmer realized that his new "Miracle Medicine" was nothing but snake oil, it was too late. The traveling huckster had beat it to the next town.

A medicine salesman at a country fair

Traveling medicine sellers sold bottles of "Jo-He Magnetic Oil" and "Wizard Oil" to cure arthritis, sore feet, rheumatism, and head colds. Fast-talking "professors" and "docs" persuaded people to buy remedies for 75 cents a bottle.

Traveling medicine sellers often worked with a musician or dancer who could draw a crowd. Medicine shows sometimes worked under tents and featured sword swallowers, magic acts, and trick shooting. "Spiritualists" worked the crowd and "spoke" to ghosts of departed loved ones. The more magical, the better. After all, the medicines promised miracle cures for aches and pains.

Camels pull a circus wagon into town

Not all traveling peddlers and entertainers were quacks. Circuses rolled across the Plains offering pure entertainment and nothing else. Families paid 75 cents for adults and 50 cents for children to see the "Great Wagon Show" or the "Great International Circus."

Acrobats, jugglers, and clowns from far-away Italy and France walked highwires, rode bareback, and juggled bowling balls. Homesteaders sat wide-eyed, glad for the distraction from work. Grady's American Circus had about fifty performers and drew crowds with their hot-air balloon show.

Traveling salesmen and peddlers sold goods door to door. Wagons were loaded with wares—fabrics, socks, bedsheets, sewing thread, and yarn. Knife and blade grinders roamed the sod frontier sharpening farmers' tools. Fruit tree peddlers sold half-dead plum and cherry trees. Booksellers sold Bibles, dictionaries, and the collected works of Shakespeare. Agents for windmill, sewing machine, and lightning rod companies offered "once in a lifetime deals."

Traveling photographers rode portable darkrooms on wheels from homestead to homestead. Even poor families would scrape up the fee to be photographed in front of their sodhouse. Peddlers sometimes traded for meals or lodging.

Traveling salesmen filled a need on the sod frontier for goods and services. However, the goods weren't always "good" and the service often a swindle.

The Bettmann Archive

Posters advertised circus shows

CROOKED HORSE TRADERS

Horse traders made the rounds of homesteads and frontier towns. They often sold horses that looked good but later proved worthless. It wasn't always easy for a farmer to tell, until he hitched the horse to a plow or saddled it up. By then it was too late. The trader was gone to the next homestead. Crooked horse traders also tricked sodbusters into horse racing contests. The trader rode into town on a horse that seemed slow or half-lame. He challenged local men to a race and took bets. Then his horse took off like a shot—no longer lame—and won! He'd trained it to "act" slow until race time.

39

Commerce on the Plains

The Plains Indians had lived and worked on the Plains for centuries before the homesteaders came. Whatever they needed, they made for themselves or found in nature. They didn't produce goods for sale in large quantities. They didn't engage in commerce as a way of life.

Pioneer cattlemen, sodbusters, and merchants brought a different way of life to the Plains. Cattlemen were the first to do business on the grasslands. Texas cowboys drove cattle to railroad stations in Kansas for shipment back East. The open range of the Great Plains became cattle country in the 1870s. By this period railroads spanned the Plains from east to west, and train cars carried cattle to market.

Railroads also brought land-hungry homesteaders and merchants to the western Plains. Homesteaders sought to make a living farming the land. Merchants and craftsmen sought to make a living by selling goods and services to the homesteaders.

Other businesses grew up as homesteaders settled the West. Millwrights ran mills for grinding grain. After a farmer harvested his wheat or corn, he needed to grind it into flour or meal. This was done by the local millwright, who ground a farmer's grain for a portion of the flour or for 25 cents a bushel.

Loading cattle onto railroad cars

The Bettmann Archive

Mills were powered by water or horses and ground grain 24 hours a day. A farmer brought his own sacks to fill with flour. Mills could process three hundred or more bushels of grain a day.

Towns and homesteads were often settled close to an existing mill. By 1860 Kansas had 36 mills, and Nebraska had 17. When millwrights sought to locate a new mill, townspeople tried to bribe them into choosing their town. This was because mills attracted farmers from miles around. And farmers brought trade to town.

HOUSEHOLD FARMS

Giant bonanza wheat farms hired hundreds of laborers to work their fields. In years when wheat prices dropped, however, bonanza farms lost their profits. Worried investors soon sold out to small-time wheat growers. Homestead families worked their own fields and kept farm costs down. They suffered through droughts and learned to grow wheat more cheaply than the bonanza growers. Neighbors shared gang plows, harvesters, and combines. In tough times and lean years, they tightened their belts—and plowed on.

Farmhands gather around a threshing machine

Sodbusters conducted other business while waiting for their grain to be ground into flour. Blacksmiths shoed horses and repaired wagons. Harness makers built and repaired saddles and harnesses. Farm equipment and supply dealers sold the latest labor-saving machinery.

Wagon builders also set up shop on the Plains frontier. So did boot makers, creameries, and hat makers. Soap makers used the meat fat they got from slaughterhouses. One Kansas soap factory turned out 200,000 pounds of soap in a year. Manufactured laundry soap saved Plains women the time and trouble of making their own.

In the 1880s and 1890s, the cattle business on the Plains gave way to a new enterprise—wheat growing. Cattle companies such as the 3 million acre XIT ranch sold grazing land to homesteading farmers. Bonanza wheat farms prospered in the Red River Valley of the Dakotas. Sodbusters and railroad men went into the wheat business.

Farms that used machines covered thousands of acres and harvested train loads of wheat bound for the U.S. and world markets. Oliver Dalrymple developed 32,000 acres of North Dakota plains for wheat growing. He employed as many as a thousand men to harvest his wheat fields.

General stores sold a wide variety of goods to townsfolk and farmers

Plains Ecology

The grasslands, river valleys, animals, and plants of the Great Plains are an ecosystem, or living environment. Each part of an ecosystem depends on the other parts. For instance, Plains animals feed on plants, insects, and other animals to survive.

All living things need fresh air, soil, and water. If soil is damaged or if water is polluted, plants can't grow. Without plants and drinking water, animals can't live. The Great Plains supported life long before humans moved there.

People first came to the Plains 30,000 years ago. Humans began changing the Plains long before the coming of homesteaders. They hunted prehistoric animals and killed off the largest ones. The buffalo managed to survive. But their days were numbered. Prehistoric Plains people also killed off ancient forests with fire.

A man sits atop a mound of buffalo hides, 1878

By the 1500s, Plains Indians were living in balance with their environment. They hunted buffalo, elk, rabbits, and other animals on foot. They took what they needed from nature and left the rest alone. Soon after white settlers arrived on the Plains, this balance was destroyed.

Spanish settlers brought horses and cattle from Mexico. These animals competed with native buffalo for food and water. In the 1860s, Texas cattle herds covered the Plains. Cowboys herded cattle on trail drives from Texas to Kansas railroads. But cattle herds overgrazed the Plains, eating most of the buffalo grasses. Few plants were left for other animals to eat. Many died or left in search of food.

Many modern Plains farmers irrigate large farms such as this one

Native Americans were also driven off the Plains or killed. Thousands died from diseases brought by white people. Their food supply, the buffalo, was wiped out. Herds were killed to make room for more cattle, railroads, and homesteads. Indians defended their lands and hunting grounds, but were defeated by settlers and the U.S. Army. By the 1880s, the Great Plains was a land of cattle, sheep, and farms. Sodbusters came to plow the Plains and change the grasslands into wheat and corn fields. Early homesteaders plowed and planted and waited for rain. Sometimes it came—other times it didn't. Farmers needed new ways to farm the dry Plains.

Homesteaders dug wells and built irrigation systems to bring water to their crops. They also planted seeds that could grow with little water. Wheat fields boomed in North Dakota and Montana. The grasslands of western Kansas were planted with fields of wheat. However, the Great Plains ecosystem was changed.

Homesteaders with ranches and cattle planted new grasses to replace the old buffalo grass. These plants brought new diseases. Plains plants were weakened by disease and died.

CHEMICAL VS. ORGANIC FARMING

Farmers have to keep soil fertile—rich in minerals—in order to grow crops. They also have to stop insects from eating crops. Most modern farms use chemicals to fertilize soil and to kill insect pests. However, chemicals also poison our air, water, and soil. Modern organic farmers use no chemicals. They use a method called crop rotation to keep the soil healthy. Crops are planted in three-year cycles with a different crop each year. This saves minerals and stops a buildup of insects.

Releasing chemicals onto fields is called crop dusting

The Plains suffered bad droughts in the 1880s and 1890s. Homesteaders dug in and stayed or left the Plains for good. In time, however, crops grew again.

Wheat fields boomed in the early 1900s. Great Plains farmers supplied wheat to the world during World War I. Sodbusters busted more and more sod, and planted more and more fields. They tore away the layer of matted grasses that protected the Plains like a skin. This exposed the soil below to erosion. Erosion occurs when soil is worn away by wind or rain.

Drought struck hard in 1931 and the land dried up. Soil hardened and cracked in dry winds. By 1935, wheat fields on the old sod frontier had turned to dust. Windstorms picked up the dust and tore across the Plains. The southern Great Plains became a "Dust Bowl." A column of dust 500 miles long and 250 miles wide whipped over the Plains and blotted out the sun. The dust didn't settle until 1939. By that time, Plains farmers had learned from their mistakes. They developed new ways of farming to stop soil erosion. Farmers learned to protect soil by planting rows of trees called windbreaks. Windbreaks help stop wind from blowing away soil. Farmers also covered soil with straw called mulch to keep moisture in and wind out.

During the Dust Bowl of the 1930s, many families abandoned their farms

Homesteaders developed these and other methods to save their land and farms. In modern times, farmers continue to face problems growing crops on the dry plains. For Great Plains farms to survive, soil and water must not be wasted. As the world's population continues to grow, Plains farmers will need to produce bountiful harvests.

INDEX